A Children's Book About

TEASING

Grolier Enterprises, Inc. offers a varied selection of children's
book racks and tote bags. For details on ordering, please write:
Grolier Enterprises Inc., Sherman Turnpike, Danbury, CT 06816
Attn: Premium Department

Managing Editor: Ellen Klarberg
Copy Editor: Annette Gooch
Editorial Assistant: Lana Eberhard
Art Director: Jennifer Wiezel
Production Artist: Susie Hornig
Illustration Designer: Bartholomew
Inking Artist: Susie Hornig
Coloring Artist: Susie Hornig
Lettering Artist: Linda Hanney
Typographer: Communication Graphics

Printed in 1990

A Children's Book About

TEASING

By Joy Berry

GROLIER ENTERPRISES CORP.

This book is about T. J. and his sister, Tami.

Reading about T. J. and Tami can help you understand and deal with **teasing.**

People are teasing you when they annoy you or make fun of you in playful ways.

Has anyone ever teased you about the way you *look*?

Has anyone ever teased you about the way you *think* and *feel*?

Has anyone ever teased you about what you *say* or *do*?

Has anyone ever teased you about what
you *like* and *do not like*?

When someone teases you, you might feel frustrated and embarrassed.

You might get upset and become angry.

People who tease often enjoy frustrating and embarrassing others.

They enjoy upsetting others.

Thus, you encourage them to continue teasing you when you become frustrated, embarrassed, or upset.

Do not become frustrated, embarrassed, or upset if you want someone who is teasing you to stop.

Do these things instead:
- Ignore anyone who teases you.
- Walk away from the person if you cannot ignore him or her.
- Do not stay around anyone who continues to tease you.

It is important to treat others the way you want to be treated.

If you do not like being teased, you should not tease others.

Try not to tease.

Do not discuss another person's private thoughts or feelings unless you have the person's permission to do so.

Try not to tease. ——————————

Do not say embarrassing things about anyone in front of others.

Try not to tease.

Avoid saying things that might hurt someone else's feelings.

This is a good rule to follow:
If you cannot say something nice about someone, avoid saying anything at all.

If you follow this rule, you will avoid hurting other people's feelings.

It is important to treat other people the way you want to be treated.

If you do not want to be teased, you should not tease others.